Giving Up on Democracy
Why Term Limits
Are Bad for America

Giving Up on Democracy

Why Term Limits Are Bad for America

Victor Kamber

Prefaces by
Sen. Bob Kerrey
& Rep. Henry Hyde

Regnery Publishing, Inc.
Washington, DC

Library of Congress Cataloging-in-Publication Data

Kamber, Victor
    Giving up on Democracy : why term limits are bad for America /
Victor Kamber ; prefaces by Bob Kerrey and Henry Hyde.
        p.   cm.
    Includes bibliographical references and index.
    ISBN 0-89526-465-X
    1. United States. Congress-Term of office. 1. Title
JJK1140.K36 1995
328.73'073-dc20

Published in the United States by
Regnery Publishing, Inc.
An Eagle Publishing Company
422 First Street, SE, Suite 300
Washington, DC 20003

Distributed to the trade by
National Book Network
4720-A Boston Way
Lanham, MD 20706

Printed on acid-free paper.
Manufactured in the United States of America

10 9 8 7 6 5 4 3 2 1

Books are available in quantity for promotional or premium use. Write to
Director of Special Sales, Regnery Publishing, Inc., 422 First Street, SE,
Suite 300, Washington, DC 20003, for information on discounts and terms or
call (202) 546-5005.

Contents

Acknowledgments

GIVING UP ON DEMOCRACY would not have been possible without the support, creativity, and wisdom of many people, too numerous to mention on a single page. Chief among them are:

Larry Hansen. A close friend dating back to our days at the University of Illinois, Larry contributed immeasurably to a 1991 White Paper, "Modern Day Snake Oil: Term Limitations and Why They Must Be Defeated," which was the precursor to *Giving Up on Democracy*. He also made similar contributions to a draft paper, "A Capital Showdown," that provided the basis for chapters 17 and 18 on constitutional issues. As someone whose life work has ranged from Capitol Hill to the halls of academia, and now to the Joyce Foundation in Chicago, Larry's insights and his passion for democracy greatly influenced this book.

Steve Weeks. A man of exceptional talents, a keen mind, and a love of language, Steve helped to turn *Giving Up on Democracy* from a concept into a reality. His ideas, creative spark, and hard work shaped this book in many ways, and I am indebted to him for his assistance.

Bruce Kozarsky. A senior vice president and director of editorial services at my communications consulting and public relations firm, The Kamber Group, Bruce played a key role in editing *Giving Up on Democracy*. His oversight, knowledge of my perspective on term limits and other issues, and wordsmithing skills were invaluable.

Many other employees of The Kamber Group and our campaign consulting subsidiary, Politics, Inc., were essential to the book's successful completion. Mark Marrow, our researcher, logged innumerable hours tracking down information and cites, checking facts, and performing other vital services. His predecessor, Ellen Conte, also provided important research for "A Capital Showdown," and Anita Cosgrove provided editorial assistance. Media Relations Director Enid Doggett, Ali Klein, Tina Dreyfus, Stacy Beck, David Rabin, and Eugene Deehan worked long and hard on promotion and publicity. Baxter Peffer performed a similar role when "Modern Day Snake Oil" was released. Throughout this period, my longtime executive assistant, Julie Speece, provided her usual indispensable support in every conceivable way. And while there is not the space to acknowledge everyone else individually, I want to thank every current and former employee of The Kamber Group who, over the past five years, offered the help, advice, and support without which *Giving Up on Democracy* would never have made it to print.

I also want to thank Richard Vigilante of Regnery Publishing for his interest in this book, his willingness to take a chance on a first-time author from the opposite side of the political spectrum, and his overall assistance in seeing this project through. Patricia Bozell of Regnery performed an elegant copyedit, and Managing Editor Jamila Abdelghani and editorial assistant David Dortman saw me and my book through the publishing process safely and securely.

Finally, I want to thank House Judiciary Committee Chair Henry Hyde and Senator Bob Kerrey for their leadership in the fight against term limits and for taking the time out of their busy schedules to write the prefaces for this book. Their passionate defense of Americans' democratic rights has earned them the respect of Americans of all political stripes who understand that, whether they agree with them or not on a particular issue, Congressman Hyde and Senator Kerrey are men of principle and integrity.

Preface

AMERICA'S VOTERS ARE ANGRY. They're fed up with a national debt nearing $5 trillion, Social Security and Medicare systems that badly need reform, and a standard of living that is stagnant at best. They're angry at hearing partisan bickering substitute for thoughtful dialogue on the issues affecting their daily lives, tired of leaders who search for enemies rather than common ground, and turned off by the irresponsible negative advertising that dominates the airwaves as election day nears.

In the face of this outrage, it is understandable that term limits have gained such popularity. But in the words of H. L. Mencken, "The cure for the evils of democracy is more democracy." And term limits would give us less democracy.

In this book, Victor Kamber lays out a cogent case for why the impulse for term limits is no substitute for a renewed commitment to citizen involvement. His recounting of the history of the term limits movement, from its inception through the 1992 and 1994 elections, in which its fundamental goal of change was achieved, should be mandatory reading for those on either side of the debate. Those whose frustration with American government created the drive for term limits should follow Kamber's prescription for changing our country through the principle that inspired its creation and sustained it through two turbulent centuries: a vibrant democracy fueled by an involved citizenry.

Voters should take their anger and channel it into activism. If politicians know that the voters will kick them out of office if they don't produce balanced budgets or improve the quality of education, then Congress will act on these issues. And if politicians know that they will be returned to office by an informed, involved electorate for doing the right thing, then that is what they will do.

The incentives and disincentives that drive our democratic process disappear with term limits. The connection between voters' wishes and elected officials' actions will be frayed beyond repair.

Strengthening this connection requires more democracy. But that requires citizens to recognize that democracy crashes on autopilot—it flies only when we take the controls.

That means staying informed about the issues and the actions of your elected representatives; cutting through the cynicism that dominates so much of the media and popular culture to find out what's really happening; being willing to make tough choices yourself about government spending, taxation, and budget deficits; and writing and calling your representatives about the issues that concern you. Above all, it means going into the voting booth on election day and pulling the lever or punching the card for the person you believe will do the best job.

If all the negative energy of the term limits movement were channeled into these positive actions, then instead of "Giving Up on Democracy," we could experience its rebirth. And the dividends—reformed, responsive government—would benefit Americans for generations to come.

Senator Bob Kerrey

IT SEEMS THE CONTENTIOUS ISSUE of term limits for elected officials has become a "brooding omnipresence" over the legislatures of our land, and most of the agitation for the dubious proposition is going unanswered. Thus, this volume by Victor Kamber is more than just timely and welcome, it is essential.

Our citizens must act thoughtfully and deliberatively in assessing the merits of such a drastic political change if we are not to permanently damage democracy itself.

Term limits fervor rests on the misconceived notion that government doesn't work very well because out-of-touch politicians refuse to pay attention to the folks back home. Someone has to tell the electorate, however, that the horrendous deficit we all complain about is the result of most Americans demanding incompatible things, such as generous federal programs *and* lower taxes. Politicians tend to give the electorate what they want. Term limits advocates' easy answer is to rotate these office holders regularly and somehow this inconsistency will disappear. I don't believe it, and anyone with even a slight grasp of human nature ought not believe it either.

In a confusing and technologically driven world, political leadership of the highest order is increasingly required. Term limits can only discourage men and women of mature judgment and experience from interrupting their careers to complete a short sabbatical in Congress. This is no part-time job.

The task of public service is a demanding one, and the complexities of a modern industrial society don't lessen as we approach the next century. In most important vocations, knowledge and experience are assets, not liabilities. Why should government be different? Of course, all elected officials are not James Madison, but the useless ones are shortly disposed of in the next election. (See November 8, 1994, if you doubt that.)

Career politicians have been accused of arrogance—but there is a whiff of arrogance in the assumption that hobbyist legislators, innocent of foreign policy, constitutional interpretations, the regulatory morass, environmental law, and weapons systems, to say nothing of budgeting or the ways of the permanent bureaucracy, can deal with these difficult problems as effectively as those with experience.

Another habit of thought that dominates the term limit mystique is the collectivization of all incumbents into one inept lump. One prominent Republican sponsor of such a bill asked what great things incumbents had done for this country, the deficit, or the huge national debt. Why is it so difficult for him and so many like him to make distinctions? Some in Congress are big spenders and high taxers, while others are the opposite. This homogenization of every incumbent has the advantage of being simplistic, but when the question is whether or not to limit the free choice of the American voter, simplicity is no virtue.

The right to vote is the heart and soul of our democratic system. Victor Kamber's spirited defense of that right would make our founding fathers, who rejected this unfettered idea, very proud.

Henry J. Hyde, M.C.

Giving Up on Democracy
Why Term Limits
Are Bad for America

Chapter **1**

Oklahoma—
Where Term Limits Came
Sweeping Down the Plains

THE FOLKS IN OKLAHOMA were frustrated. Ever since the oil bust, the economy had been moribund. All they had got out of that spending spree known as the 1980s were some strip malls that had run the old mom-and-pop stores out of business and ruined the Main Streets of small towns. Also, there were some shiny new office buildings in Oklahoma City and Tulsa, but a lot of them were vacant now. The oil barons who had gotten rich off Oklahoma during the good years didn't leave much behind when they left. The manufacturing jobs had gone south down to Mexico, where the labor was cheaper and you didn't have to follow strict safety standards. The Sooners were coming off another disappointing football season. It was a tough time to be an Okie.

Then the state legislators started playing games. They couldn't finish all their business during the constitutionally limited session, so they simply stopped the clock in the capital and argued that the legislative day hadn't yet ended. Shortly after that, they got a tremendous pay raise of $32,000 (more than most Oklahomans made in a year) for only three months' work. After that some renegade Democrats and minority Republicans unseated the popular Speaker of the House.

The people wanted the economy back on track, the state government cleaned up, the schools improved, and drugs and crime brought under control. But nothing seemed to be working. What was once a healthy skepticism toward politics became a deep and vehement dissatisfaction.

THE FIRST CAMPAIGN

So when a couple of wealthy businessmen started talking about term limits for Oklahoma state legislators, they had an audience that was willing to listen and eager to agree. In the beginning, only a few people in Oklahoma wanted term limits. But one of them was a millionaire, and the other was a billionaire who happened to own the state's largest newspaper.

Oklahoma is a one-newspaper state. The *Daily Oklahoman* calls itself "The statewide newspaper since 1907." It's published by Edward L. Gaylord, who is the richest person in the state. Gaylord uses his newspaper to promote his extremely conservative political views. He constantly attacks the Democrat-controlled state legislature in front-page editorials in his paper, which is read throughout the state. The only real competition Gaylord faces is from a local daily in the Tulsa area.

Gaylord and his publishing company gave large contributions to committees whose missions were to promote ballot initiatives, including one for term limits. In addition to helping out with cash, Gaylord supported the term limits initiative in his editorials—which never mentioned that Gaylord was a major contributor to the cause.

The other power behind term limits was Lloyd Noble II. A self-described "arch-conservative," Noble is a wealthy Tulsa oilman whose family is involved in various philanthropic endeavors. Noble, once an unsuccessful candidate for the state legislature, had a strong commitment to term limits. He knew that a term limits law would never get through that body but could be passed in an initiative. He wanted the initiative to win in Oklahoma so that the nascent term limits movement could gain support throughout the country.

Noble hired a political consulting firm in Oklahoma City to conduct a poll measuring the popular support for term limits. Although the issue was fairly new and unfamiliar to many voters, the poll results were strong enough to convince Noble to begin the initiative process.

He gathered some political pros together to draft a petition to the secretary of state. The petition was carefully worded, and while twelve-year term limits were imposed on state representatives and senators, it left the federal delegation alone.

The next step was for Noble to get the signatures he needed to put the petition on the ballot. He hired paid collectors to gather more than 175,000 signatures within ninety days. Once the signatures were collected and validated, Noble persuaded the Republican governor (whose party colleagues had a vested interest in term-limiting the Democrat-controlled House) to place the petition on the primary run-off ballot in September 1990, rather than wait for the November general election. Turnout is lower in primary elections—especially runoffs—which meant Noble could count on committed and active supporters getting out to vote while most of the public stayed home. If the bill passed, it would make Oklahoma the first state to impose term limits on its legislature. And being on the primary run-off ballot would allow candidates to avoid taking a public stand on the issue, since many of them either had no primary opponent or had averted a runoff by winning more than 50 percent of the votes. They wouldn't, therefore, have to campaign either for or against term limits.

Noble supplied most of the $220,000 budget for his organization, Oklahomans for Legislative Reform. He had a bipartisan cast of supporting politicians, including Cleta Deatherage Mitchell, a former Oklahoma Democratic state legislator, who lost a race for lieutenant governor and now heads the Term Limits Legal Institute; former Governor Raymond Gary; and most of the Republican minority in the House. Democratic gubernatorial candidate David Walters also strongly supported the initiative and gave the issue free publicity in many of his campaign ads. Walters had initially offered to support the initiative in return for Noble's endorsement, but Noble had turned him down.

With Gaylord's editorials, Walters' campaign ads, and Noble's own media buys, term limits was the most highly publicized issue in the primary. Despite the importance of the initiative and the great noise it generated, there was very little debate. According to political scientist Gary Copeland, "from the campaign waged in Oklahoma no one would guess that such a weighty issue was before the voters."[1]

An antiterm limits group called the Committee to Protect the Rights of Oklahoma Voters (PROVE) was hastily assembled. Its members raised and spent less than one-quarter of what Noble spent on his drive. The most visible opponent of term limits was retired House Speaker Carl Albert, but even his contribution was too little, too late.

Voters approved the initiative by an almost two-to-one margin on September 18, 1990, and Oklahoma got bragging rights as the first state to adopt term limits. Other states soon followed. California and Colorado both had successful term limits measures on their 1990 ballots, and the term limits movement went on to become a national phenomenon. Twenty-three states passed some form of term limits legislation, either by voter initiative or through the state legislature. Those laws were effectively invalidated by the recent Supreme Court decision, but that doesn't mean the fight over term limits is over. Not by a long shot.

THE PROBLEM WITH TERM LIMITS

While term limits may sound like a good idea, they're actually a big mistake. Soon we will begin to see the effects of this disruptive and misguided attempt to short-circuit democracy. But in California and some other states that have imposed term limits, there have already been signs of political chaos and a dangerous power shift away from elected representatives and toward unelected lobbyists and bureaucrats.

By voting for term limits, Oklahomans abdicated their right to elect representatives of their own choosing. They turned to a quick, legalistic fix instead of making the hard choices necessary to bring about real change. They handed their government over to the special interests and bureaucracy. They made elections less competitive and less fair.

But they weren't warned of all of these consequences before they went to the polls. The debate over term limits has been undertaken in an atmosphere of anger and hysteria, and the voters have not been given the facts concerning this most important issue.

Term limits supporters have called themselves "the greatest grassroots movement in American history." But, in fact, the movement has been initiated and financed by a few rich and powerful men. Yes, many people have already voted for term limits, and yes, when asked by pollsters, a majority favor limiting political terms of office. But the term limits movement can hardly be called grassroots.

I believe that when the voters hear the truth about term limits, they will decide that limiting their representatives' terms is nothing less than giving up on democracy. In the meantime, the term limits movement is spreading like a prairie fire, and if we don't put it out, we're all going to get burned.

Chapter 2

Mandatory Rotation: The History of a Bad Idea

The people are the best judge who ought to represent them. To dictate and control them, to tell them whom they shall elect, is to abridge their natural rights.

—Robert Livingston

LIKE MANY OTHER BAD IDEAS, term limits has been around a long time. In fact, we've already had term limits, and they didn't work.

After winning independence from England and before crafting the Constitution, Americans established a government under the Articles of Confederation. Because the former British subjects were suspicious of centralized power, they instituted a weak central government, with most of the power residing in the states. The only federal governmental body created by the Articles was the Continental Congress, but it could do nothing without the approval of at least nine of the thirteen states. The Continental Congress could not tax or regulate commerce, and although it could "requisition" money, it had no power to collect it. Another restraint on the body's power, which ultimately proved crippling, was term limits.

The result of term limits was a system of independent states under a dangerously weak central government. The economic and political crises resulting from this lack of central power threatened the stability, even the viability, of the new republic. Armed insurrections, including Shay's Rebellion, during which starving veterans of the Revolutionary Army marched on Boston, led the nation's leaders to reconsider such a loosely organized confederation of states.

The issue of term limits was not the only problem with the Articles of Confederation, but it was particularly nettlesome. The Articles restricted congressional service to three consecutive terms in any six-year period. And the legislative body established by the Articles was by no means democratic. Members of the Continental Congress were appointed by state legislatures, were issued precise instructions on how to vote, and could be recalled at any time and for any reason—and occasionally were. Congress did not represent the public; it represented state governments, whose overriding concern was to preserve their autonomy from the central government.

When John Fund of the *Wall Street Journal* argues that the Articles of Confederation included term limits in order "to ensure that legislators reflected the makeup and outlook of the citizens they claimed to represent,"[1] he fundamentally misrepresents the forces that were at work during the country's formative years. Members of the Continental Congress were kept on short leashes to protect the interests of the states, not to reflect popular opinion. Term limits were a way of maintaining parity among the states by making it difficult for the legislators of any one state to gain more power than any other. They were not designed to make the legislators more responsive to the people, who didn't elect them anyway.

In advertising the Articles of Confederation as precedent, the advocates of term limits understandably gloss over another equally important point. In March 1784, opposition to congressional limits became so powerful that the leaders of the Continental Congress finally refused to enforce them. One of the most perverse effects of these early term limits was that the continued service of extraordinary men like James Madison was suspended just when their talents were most urgently needed.

The experience with the Articles of Confederation shows that term limits are impractical. In his *Commentaries on the Constitution*, eminent legal scholar and Supreme Court Justice Joseph Story noted that the limitations provision in the Articles of Confederation had caused:

> too frequent rotation... in the office of members of Congress, by which the advantages, resulting from experience and knowledge in the public affairs, were lost to the public councils.[2]

It was a lesson the drafters of the Constitution did not forget when they got down to work in Philadelphia in 1787.

THE CONSTITUTIONAL DEBATE OVER TERM LIMITS

Despite the difficulties caused by term limits in the Articles, the first draft of the Constitution presented at the opening of the Constitutional Convention did have a provision for them. The "Virginia Plan" would have barred members of the House of Representatives from office for an unspecified number of years after their terms expired. But that provision was quickly, and *unanimously*, deleted.

Term limits supporters tend to skip rather prettily over the facts when discussing the constitutional debate on term limits. They want to say that term limits were supported by the Framers of the Constitution, when in fact they were not. John Fund says that term limits "were left out of the Constitution largely because it was thought of as 'entering too much detail' for a short document."[3]

This is an uncharitable and inaccurate reading of the Framers' motivations in this matter. These were not men inclined to overlook details, when they thought details were important. The addition of a few short sentences to Article I would have done the trick. But they had learned from bitter experience that term limits only caused problems and didn't solve any.

The Framers of the Constitution wanted experienced legislators who would use their wisdom and expertise to provide leadership for the fledgling country. They had no objections to politicians being repeatedly returned to office, as long as they performed honestly and effectively and maintained their voters' support. In *The Federalist* No. 53, Madison explained the convention's rationale:

> A few of the members [of Congress]... will possess superior talents; will by frequent reelections, become members of long standing; will be thoroughly masters of the public business, and perhaps not unwilling to avail themselves of those advantages.[4]

The convention's reasoning for excluding limits is as powerful and relevant today as it was two hundred years ago. Despite their attempts to link term limits to the original intent of the Framers of the Constitution, the term limiters cannot dress up history enough to alter the basic facts.

THE CASE AGAINST TERM LIMITS

Why did the Framers of the Constitution reject term limits? Because they believed that frequent elections were a form of natural term limits: they required legislators to go repeatedly before the voters to earn their support. Frequent elections were the best way to prevent abuse of power by Congress. James Madison called regular elections "the cornerstone of liberty," and argued in *The Federalist Papers* that effective legislators should be returned to office frequently. He believed that experience was necessary for a legislator to perform in the people's best interests:

> No man can be a competent legislator who does not add to an upright intention and a sound judgment a certain degree of knowledge of the subjects on which he is to legislate. A part of this knowledge may be acquired by means of information which lies within the compass of men in private as well as public stations. Another part can only be attained, or at least thoroughly attained, by actual experience in the station which requires the use of it.[5]

While the proponents of term limits sneer at "professional politicians," the Framers of our Constitution thought that experienced and capable legislators were the best guarantors of freedom. And they were wary of inexperienced legislators. "The greater the proportion of new members, and the less the information of the bulk of the members, the more apt will they be to fall into the snares that may be laid for them," argued the writers of *The Federalist*.[6]

Term limits are specifically addressed in *The Federalist* No. 72, written by Alexander Hamilton, whose understanding of what motivated politicians was so uncanny that one might speculate such wisdom came from self-reflection as well as observation. He felt that one ill effect of term limits would be "a diminution of the inducements to good behavior. There are few men who would not feel much less zeal in the discharge of a duty, when they were conscious that the advantages of the station with which it was connected must be relinquished at a determinate period."[7]

Hamilton was no Pollyanna; he knew that "the desire for reward is one of the strongest incentives of human conduct... the best security for the fidelity of mankind is to make their interest coincide with their duty."[8] Term limits would reduce the rewards for public service, since leaders would not be able to see their policies through and, therefore, would either find their agendas unfulfilled or would get no credit for them if they were ultimately enacted.

Imagine if you were given a job and told that you will be taken off the job at a certain point in time, no matter how well you do it. What will be your incentive to work hard? In the same way, if legislators are allotted only a certain number of terms and are not able to see many of their goals achieved, they will have little incentive to do more than keep their seats warm and show up for roll call votes. Or worse, they can wreak havoc, since they won't be around to suffer the consequences.

Open elections have the positive incentives that Hamilton mentions, giving legislators the opportunity to pursue their ambitions. And they also create negative incentives—if a politician does not perform or violates the public trust, the people can throw him or her out of office.

Madison correctly saw the reelection process as a means of popular discipline, accountability, and control of elected officials. "[Officeholders] will be compelled to anticipate the moment when their power is to cease, when their exercise of it is to be reviewed, and when they must descend to the level from which they are raised; there forever to remain *unless* a faithful discharge of their trust have established their title to a *renewal* of it."[9]

Hamilton also saw the temptations that would result from a mandatory limit on officeholding. Even a venal or ambitious legislator who is facing a reelection would not take as much advantage of the office as he would if he knew he were leaving, never to return. As Hamilton put it, "His avarice might be a guard against his avarice."[10]

Experience was also crucial to Hamilton. "That experience is the parent of wisdom, is an adage the truth of which is recognized by the wisest as well as the simplest of mankind. What more desirable or more essential than this quality in the governors of nations?"[11]

During the debate for ratification in his home state of New York, Hamilton repeatedly made the following points:

1. The people have the right to judge whom they will and will not elect to public office.

2. Rotation reduces the incentives for political accountability.

3. Rotation deprives the polity of experienced public servants.[12]

These arguments were powerful enough in their time to convince the delegates to reject term limits. Their strength has not diminished in the two centuries since they were composed.

RELEGATED TO THE MARGINS

Despite their defeat in the Constitutional Convention, term limits did not go away immediately. In the first session of the newly established Congress, several proposals were offered to restrict representatives to six consecutive years in any eight-year period. But these proposals were in turn soundly defeated and the issue finally put to rest.

The next attempts to alter the terms set down in the Constitution came from the opposite direction. Representatives began pressing for longer terms, to lessen the pressures of campaigning and establish more career stability in the House. Amendments proposing longer terms were introduced in every session after 1869. There were sixty-four such proposals between 1929 and 1963. During that same period, only nine attempts were made to limit terms.

Texas Senator W. Lee "Pappy" O'Daniel introduced a plan in 1948 to limit the president and all of Congress to a single six-year term. His proposal was defeated by a margin of 82–1.

In the wake of Vietnam and Watergate, lawmakers introduced several bills either to limit terms of office or to increase a representative's term to four years. In 1978, a Senate Judiciary subcommittee even held hearings on term limits. Two of the sponsors of term limit amendments were Senators John Danforth (R-Mo.) and Dennis DeConcini (D-Ariz.), both of whom served eighteen years in office. Dan Quayle's first speech on the House floor was in support of term limits.

For a long time, term limits were a marginal issue, supported only by idiosyncratic politicians who knew (and probably hoped) that their proposals would never be passed.

COMING TO A LEGISLATURE NEAR YOU

Now all of a sudden the issue of term limits has returned, more radical and more popular than ever. Why is that?

People are frustrated with the political system. There are many problems that seem insoluble, and Congress at times does not appear willing to address them effectively. Drugs, crime, the economy, health care, the looming crises in Social Security and Medicare, the federal deficit, the breakdown of our schools and other public institutions—all these are serious and dramatic problems, and the American people are justly worried about them.

But term limits aren't going to make things any better. They're only going to make these problems even more difficult to address politically. With a Congress hampered by term limits and filled with rookie legislators still learning the ropes and short-term "veterans" angling for jobs when their terms run out, it will be next to impossible to get meaningful and effective legislation out of Congress.

Despite the historical record, term limits are being sold as a quick and painless cure to everything that ails our body politic. The people behind term limits are promising one easy solution to a variety of complex problems. The Framers knew that there are no quick fixes, and they found out the hard way that term limits do not deliver as promised. That's why they refused to put term limits in the Constitution, and that's why we should honor their wisdom and foresight by keeping elections open to everyone, even experienced politicians.

Chapter 3

Populism or Elitism?

Democracy is like blowing your nose—you may not do it well, but you ought to do it yourself.

—G. K. Chesterton

WE ALREADY HAVE TERM LIMITS. They're called elections.

Every two years you can vote to end the term of your representative. Every six years you can vote to kick your senator out of office. No one is forcing you to vote for incumbents, but legally imposed term limits will deprive you of the right to vote for them if you want to.

What if you went to a car dealer and were told that you can buy any car that you want, as long as it isn't the same one that you had before, even if it had served you well?

What if you went into the hardware store and the salesperson said that you can get any color house paint, as long as it doesn't match the color of your house?

What if you went to the video store and the clerk told you that you can't rent "Casablanca" because you've already seen it before?

That's exactly what term limits advocates are telling you. They don't want you to make your own choices, because they assume you can't be trusted with your own vote.

POWER OVER PEOPLE

Arguments for term limits are often filled with pseudopopulist rhetoric. "The strength of our society has never been experts dictating to the people from Washington, but rather, our greatness has always been due to the common sense and the common decency of the American people. Trust the people." So says Paul Jacob, the head of U.S. Term Limits.

But behind the rhetoric is the reality: Term limits are profoundly elitist. We have already seen how a few rich and powerful people were able to convince Oklahomans to vote against their best interests and impose term limits on their state legislators. That's happened in every state where term limits have passed—a few people with their own ideological and personal motivations (joined in some cases by well-meaning but ill-informed citizens) have sold everyone else a phony bill of goods. But the elitism of term limits is about more than just money and power. It's about someone telling you how to vote.

Right now you can vote for any candidate you choose. But under term limits your right to vote for the candidate of your choice will be severely compromised. You won't be able to vote for your own representatives simply because they proved themselves popular and effective by winning previous elections.

While the supporters of term limits run the ideological gamut from the far Right (where most of them are) to the activist Left, they share one thing in common: They don't believe that you can be trusted with your vote. If they succeed in selling term limits to the rest of the country, there's no telling where it will end. Free and democratic elections are the only guarantee of liberty. Once they are compromised, our other rights are threatened.

STOP ME BEFORE I VOTE AGAIN

The issue of term limits gained prominence at a time when the rate of incumbents returning to Congress was very high. Polls showed that some three-quarters of the American people supported term limits, yet they kept reelecting the same politicians to represent them. Psychologists call this cognitive dissonance—when actions and desires are in direct contradiction to one another. There has always been a measurable degree of cognitive dissonance in American politics. It is almost a tradition in this country for people to rail against Congress as an institution while supporting the member who represents them. But with every passing day, the tenor of such complaints seems to get more and more rancorous. And now there is a mechanism by which that rancor can be translated into political action.

In the 1992 elections, voters in Arkansas passed a constitutional amendment restricting their representatives' terms. In the same election, they returned eighteen-year veteran Dale Bumpers to the Senate. Voters in Ohio also went for limited terms, and then proceeded to send three-term Senator John Glenn back to Washington. In 1994, Massachusetts voted for term limits and reelected thirty-two-year veteran Teddy Kennedy. In both election years, the return rate for running incumbents was over 90 percent.

People want term limits, but they like their incumbent congressional representatives. What does that mean? That they want to get rid of yours. They're willing to sacrifice their own representatives just so you can't reelect yours.

This is precisely the kind of tyranny that our system of checks and balances was created to prevent. The Framers did not want one region or group of people to control another, which is what will happen under term limits. By passing a constitutional amendment, other people will be telling you whom you can and cannot vote for.

WHO NEEDS ELECTIONS?

Term limiters don't like elections. They see the electoral process as corrupt, debasing, and inherently unfair. Instead of trying to reform the system, they want to recast it completely. Because it is mistakenly seen as painless rather than the radical restructuring that it actually is, term limits will derail any chances of meaningful reform.

Elections are not merely a way of selecting representatives, they are a ritual of democracy itself. Voting has a symbolic as well as a practical resonance. When you step inside the voting booth and pull the curtain closed, you are affirming and celebrating democracy.

Why not avoid the electoral process entirely and select legislators by lottery? That's been suggested by Marc Petracca, a political scientist who supports term limits. In a piece published in the *Orange County Register*, Petracca calls for sortition, or the selecting of legislators by lot. Sortition was used in ancient Athens and Rome and in Renaissance Venice to appoint political leaders from among the ranking noblemen. Petracca doesn't see why we can't choose our political leaders the same way. While he is not sanguine about the possibility of his proposal being adopted on the national level, he figures "there's no reason why states and municipalities could not begin to put the nomination rule of sortition into practice immediately."[1]

While Petracca's argument has a level of op-ed irony in it, behind his audacious proposal is an attitude shared by many term limiters. They have contempt, not just for the politicians running for office, but for the people who vote them in as well. Let's face it, term limiters do not like elections. And if someone doesn't like elections, how do you think he or she feels about democracy itself?

A PROCESS, NOT A RESULT

As people all over the world are discovering, democracy doesn't happen overnight. Effective self-government comes only at great cost and struggle, and democratic experiments often fail, despite the best intentions. America did not instantly become a democracy on July 4, 1776, when the Declaration of Independence was signed, or in 1789, when the Constitution was ratified. The creation of American democracy was a long and often painful endeavor. We fought a civil war and several political skirmishes (some violent, some bloodless) to extend democratic rights to all the people. And our country's constitutional development is the still-unfolding story of enhancing citizens' authority over their own government. Extending the franchise to former slaves and their heirs, and then to women, and then to eighteen-year–olds are important chapters in this story. The abandonment of property requirements, poll taxes, and literacy tests for voters were also significant events. So too was the decision eighty years ago to permit voters rather than state legislatures to elect U.S. senators.

The expansion of democracy hasn't ended. It can be argued that we do not now have a complete and properly functioning democracy. Voter turnout was down to 38 percent in the 1994 election. Some states' refusal to implement the "Motor Voter" Act highlights often cumbersome voter registration provisions that make it difficult for people juggling family and work responsibilities to add their names to the voter rolls. The citizens of the District of Columbia pay taxes but still have no voting representation in Congress. Money is increasingly the most decisive force in elections. In a land where the rich get richer and the powerful grow in influence, minorities and the poor are feeling increasingly marginalized.

Democracy is a process, not a result. It should be constantly refined and expanded, so that its citizens enjoy the greatest participation in their own government. Term limits will turn back the clock and reverse the process of democracy.

DEMOCRATIC RESPONSIBILITIES

Term limits do more than just damage the process of democracy; they diminish its very culture by taking away from the voters one of their most important obligations: making an informed and responsible choice on Election Day. Term limits are a way of throwing up your hands and saying that it doesn't matter who gets elected, as long as it's not the person who served before. This is a cheap and lazy way of participating in government. As *Washington Post* columnist David Broder wrote:

> The worst effect of term limits is to send a message to Americans
> that they can enjoy all the blessings of representative government

without meeting even the most fundamental responsibility of citizenship—participation in the choice of leaders. For more than two hundred years, we have changed people in office through elections. Why, in this generation, has that become such a burden that we must find some automatic, no-brains, no-bother way to do the job?[2]

In other words, term limits are a gimmick. Instead of facing up to our political obligations and making the decisions necessary to address the problems confronting our country, it is easier to pass a law that will guarantee change (for better or worse) without having to do the heavy lifting. By relying on gimmicks like term limits, the Balanced Budget Amendment, and the Gramm-Rudman-Hollings Act (which also are somehow supposed to solve all our problems with a wave of the magic wand), we are abdicating our responsibilities as citizens and allowing our representatives to avoid making the tough choices that will eventually have to be made if this country is ever going to get back on track. A government cannot run on autopilot.

No one puts a gun to your head and forces you to vote for an incumbent. What's so difficult about limiting terms the old-fashioned way, by simply voting? Just how hard is that, anyway?

We shouldn't depend on some kind of system that makes our decisions for us automatically. Not only is this dangerous in terms of policy (what will happen if a term limits experiment proves to be even more disastrous than it was under the Articles?) but it also diminishes the skills of citizenry. A democracy gives citizens the gift of freedom, but it comes at a price—the responsibility to take an active, informed role in the affairs of our country. It demands something of us, and quick-fix gimmicks like term limits do not put off the inevitable necessity of facing up to the challenges that are only temporarily put off. Term limits are more than just giving up on our elected representatives—they're giving up on democracy itself. And that's exactly what the elitists behind term limits want you to do.

Chapter 4

The Myth of Cincinnatus

A great state cannot be run by "citizen legislators" and amateur administrators.

—George Will

SINCE MAKING THAT STATEMENT, George Will has changed his mind. Now he's in favor of term limits and "citizen legislators." But I use his quote to remind him, and others, that he was right the first time.

The idea of the citizen legislator is something of a fetish among term limiters. You will hear the term in almost every argument, usually invoked as the alternative to "professional politicians." It is an empty shibboleth, never truly defined, and we are given only vague examples of who these citizen legislators would be. As Louis Menand put it: " 'Citizen legislator' is one of those phrases, like 'personal feeling,' that try to purchase some extra probity with a little redundancy."[1]

In fact, the "citizen legislator" is a myth, and a pernicious one at that. Like much of the fertilizer that the term limits movement tries to shovel on the American people, the idea of a citizen legislature is elitism disguised as populism, the arrogant voice of an aristocrat trying to sound like a democrat.

CITIZENS OR ARISTOCRATS?

What is wrong with the idea of a citizen legislature? If we mean simply a legislature made up of citizens, we already have one. But term limiters do not mean that at all. Instead they call for part-time politicians who will serve only a few years in Congress and then go back to whatever they were doing before.

There are two problems with this argument. First, it ignores the fact that public service is a calling, requiring a certain level of sacrifice and commitment, and a profession, requiring specific skills and expertise. Specialization is a reality of the modern world, and much as we may deplore the fact that few, if any, public officials can be as multitalented as Thomas Jefferson, the world is much more complex now than it was in his time.

Jefferson was said to know everything that was worth knowing. Two hundred years ago that was still possible. The amount of useful information has grown exponentially in the past two centuries, even in the past ten years. All you have to do is enter a college library or go surfing on the Internet to realize that even a superficial understanding of the complete range of human knowledge is impossible today.

At the same time as our information base has expanded, our institutions have become increasingly complex. To be an effective member of Congress, one must be expert in several different fields—say, energy and the environment and tax law—in addition to being skilled in politics. The federal budget (including appendices, tables, and other documents) is 2,215 pages long. The federal code contains 205 volumes. A legislator could not possibly develop the expertise necessary to deal intelligently with these complex issues without devoting a great deal of time and, yes, even a career to it.

The second, and to my mind more dangerous, problem with the idea of the citizen legislature is that it is a myth romanticized right out of reality. The term limiters invoke the phrase in misty reverence, summoning images of a Renaissance man putting his personal business aside to serve his nation in time of need. But the plain, simple, and unavoidable fact is that, during the Renaissance, citizen legislators were wealthy aristocrats who could put aside their personal business because they had others, often slaves, to do it for them.

THE REAL CINCINNATUS

The model of the "citizen legislator" was given to us, like many other myths, by the Romans. And the most prominent among the Roman citizen legislators was Cincinnatus, a nobleman who supposedly personified the virtues of selfless public service and patriotism.

The legend goes like this: Cincinnatus was working out in his fields when emissaries came from Rome asking him to become dictator so he could lead the fight against the Aequi, who had trapped the Roman army. He put down his plow and went to serve his country, defeating the Aequi in one day. Then he returned to Rome, where he held the position of dictator only as long as it took to guide his country through the military emergency. Once that was accomplished, he went back to his farm and again took up his plow. Years later he was given a second dictatorship to check the ambitions of one Spurius Maelius. Once again he surrendered power and once again returned to his farm when the crisis was over.

That is the legend. These are the facts: Cincinnatus was a vain and arrogant man who frequently refused or abandoned the political positions offered him because they were not powerful enough to suit his dictatorial tastes. While the myth has portrayed him as a gentleman farmer, he was a nobleman and slaveholder who would have found manual labor beneath him. If, in fact, he had been in the fields when summoned to war, he wouldn't have been behind the plow, but beating his naked, starving slaves for not working hard enough.

THE MYTH IN AMERICA

It is easy to forget that America, like ancient Rome, was once an aristocracy. And many of the American aristocrats had built their fortunes on slave labor. This is not to diminish the great achievements of our founders. Just because Jefferson and Washington owned slaves does not negate their contributions to democracy. But it is essential to have historical perspective, especially when political arguments are being made to return us to some Arcadia of the past.

How real is the myth of the citizen legislator in America? Just two out of ninety-four members elected to the first Congress were strangers to public service. Only eight of the original senators had not already been representatives in either the Continental Congress or the similar body under the Articles. Twenty members of the first Congress had helped draft the Constitution, and many were members of state-ratifying conventions. All told, most of the fifty-five Constitutional Convention delegates devoted their lifetimes to public service—as presidents, governors, legislators, jurists, cabinet officers, and foreign envoys. Those who did return to private life often did so not out of choice but out of necessity due to political defeat.

Of course, they served our country during times of crisis. But once the country stabilized, the principle of voluntary rotation came into being, partly following the example of Washington and subsequent presidents who left office after two terms, although there was no limit on the office at that time. Rotation was observed by legislators well into the nineteenth century. Men—and they were all men—came into office for a few years, after which they returned to their communities and careers. It was a self-enforcing ethic and required no laws to enforce it.

But why did these legislators leave Washington to return to their homes? Was it because they did not want to become career politicians—or were there other considerations?

First of all, members of Congress were paid very little back then. In the mid-1800s, they received just $8 a day while Congress was in session. And remember that travel was arduous in those days before the airplane and automobile. It could take weeks to travel to

Washington from their homes, where they left their families. Most congressmen lived in boarding houses. And Washington was far from the international metropolis that it is today. Pigs rooted on Pennsylvania Avenue, the stench of open sewers became unbearable in summer, and the oppressive humidity in this former swamp was unrelieved by the future invention of air conditioning. A political term in Washington was often an undesirable posting endured in order to reap greater political benefits back home. British diplomats posted to the American capital received hardship pay because the conditions were so miserable.

Abraham Lincoln, who served one term in Congress, is often advertised as an exemplar of the nineteenth-century citizen legislator. But Lincoln's two-year stint in Washington was, in fact, the result of a deal cut in the early 1840s with two other prominent Whigs, all of whom wanted to go to Congress from Illinois' only solidly Whig district. To avoid a divisive nominating convention, the three men decided each would serve for two years, with Lincoln agreeing to go last.

This arrangement was not the result of high-minded adherence to the citizen legislator ideal. Rather, it was a sensible way of reconciling the clashing ambitions of three young men eager to get ahead. Or some might less charitably call it a back-room political deal that left the voters out of the equation. (Lincoln flirted with the idea of running for a second term, but his votes against the Mexican War were so unpopular that he could not possibly have won. In 1848 his district went Democratic for the first time.)

As the nation and the government grew, and life in general became more specialized and complex, Washington politics became a career in itself—subject, of course, to the approval of the voters. Like all forms of progress, this development is not without its problems, but on the whole it has made our government stronger and our country greater. To dismiss the achievements of career politicians is to disregard some of the political changes that were essential to our nation's development and to slight another great tradition of our nation: public service.

WHO ARE THE
CITIZEN LEGISLATORS?

"If we can achieve a citizen legislature, then we will have citizens from all walks of life who will go to serve their constituents," Lloyd Noble II once said.

Mr. Noble, you may recall, is the millionaire who sold Oklahoma on the idea of term limits. And while it may be very easy for a millionaire to imagine ordinary people putting aside their careers for a shot at joining Congress, the rest of us realize that it would indeed be difficult for anyone who was not already wealthy and well connected to leave his or her job and run for office, which, for one, entails having to raise thousands, often millions, of dollars.

So the next time someone who supports term limits starts telling you about "citizen legislators," remember that his or her idea of a citizen legislator is not John Q. Public, but Citizen Kane. That egomaniacal newspaper magnate of Orson Welles' great film is precisely the kind of person who would run for office under term limits: someone who sees political leadership not as fulfilling an ethos of public service, but as a pleasant little detour in his or her career or a path to even greater power and wealth.

What kind of people would run for office under term limits? The wealthy and ambitious, those who see a long-term gain from a short-term commitment. We would see more Michael Huffingtons and Ross Perots, and fewer talented, dedicated professionals willing to devote their lives to public service. The ballots would be filled with the names of eccentric millionaires and callow trust-fund babies, arbitrageurs, and polo players.

In short, Congress would return to what it was before, a rich man's club in which those who did not have the wealth and position necessary to afford a temporary sabbatical in Washington would be excluded from the political process. That means modern-day congressional giants from humble backgrounds, like Harry Truman, Tip O'Neill, Newt Gingrich, and Phil Gramm, would have found it impractical or impossible to serve their country.

And there is a reason term limit proponents, especially those of a conservative bent, often invoke the sacred phrase "citizen legisla-tors." They want to return to the days of an American aristocracy, in which a few landed gentry not only profited off the backs of over-worked laborers and slaves, but also passed the laws to make such profits possible.

America has changed a lot in two hundred years. Democracy has evolved, and the process still continues. Congress is a much more democratic institution than it was even fifty years ago. There are now many members whose backgrounds more closely resemble that of Cincinnatus' slaves than Cincinnatus.

Term limits may indeed bring back citizen legislators. But the rich and the powerful are already well represented and don't need affirmative action. Instead of turning back the clock, we should be pressing forward. Rather than giving up on our democracy, we should be working harder to make it better.

Chapter **5**

California—
The End of the Road

California is a place in which a boom mentality and a sense of Chekhovian loss meet in uneasy suspension; in which the mind is troubled by some buried but ineradicable suspicion that things had better work here, because here, beneath that immense bleached sky, is where we run out of continent.

—Joan Didion

THE CALIFORNIA LEGISLATURE was once the model for the country, as the state itself once seemed to embody our greatest successes and highest aspirations. But California is no longer the land of golden promise, and its legislature is a mess.

In many ways California's problems resemble those of the nation as a whole. A troubled economy, fiscal crisis, racial unrest, drug abuse, the failure of the schools, implacable poverty and underemployment, natural disasters, and a general sense of frustration and uncertainty plague our largest state as much or more than the other forty-nine.

And then the people of California were told that term limits was the way to solve these problems. Unfortunately, Californians listened and passed two initiatives limiting the terms of their state and federal representatives.

Since California is the first state in which term limits will take effect (state term limits will not be affected by the May 22 Supreme Court decision against term limits) it will be observed by many as the laboratory for term limits, to see if the law lives up to its billing. But even though the first term-limited legislator won't be forced out of office until 1996, the consequences are already being felt. In California, as in the rest of the country, term limits are part of a

Election Year	Number of Members Starting Term 1	Number of Members Starting Term 2	Number of Members Starting Term 3
1996	61	10	9
1998	19	52	9
2000	19	16	44
2002	50	16	14
2004	24	42	14
2006	24	20	36
2008	42	20	17
2010	27	36	17

Source: *Karl T. Kurtz,* "Assessing the Potential Impacts of Term Limits," *State Legislatures 18, January 1992.*

larger and more troubling movement in which voters are voluntarily abdicating their rights, and thus neglecting their duties as citizens, by supporting legislative mechanisms that avoid the deliberative democratic process and enforce strict, and often harsh, measures on the government. Tax cuts, mandatory sentencing for criminals, laws requiring supermajorities for tax increases or appropriations—these are all ways of giving up on democracy and giving in to quick-fix politics. Like many other trends, it started in California.

REVOLT OF THE RICH

In 1978 California began a political revolution by passing Proposition 13, a ballot initiative that cut property taxes and eviscerated state and local government. The tax revolt movement was led by Howard Jarvis and Paul Gann, a couple of elderly conservative political activists, who convinced a lot of other Californians they were paying too much in taxes. Most of the proposition's support came from "predominantly white, politically involved, generally elderly taxpayers whose children were grown and who had only a marginal interest in schools, parks, and other local public services," according to Peter Schrag, editorial page editor of the *Sacramento Bee*.[1]

Proposition 13 shifted the financial burden from the local governments to the state, which is now unable to deliver some of the most essential services. While Proposition 13 reduced taxes for homeowners, it priced new homes out of the reach of many young families. And it required that a tax increase be passed by a two-thirds majority in the state assembly, making it easy for any well-organized interest group to block legislation. Proposition 13 had profound national impact as well. The Reagan tax cuts that created massive budget deficits and national debt were based in large part on the "success" of the California tax revolt.

Proposition 13 was just the beginning. It created a political precedent for special interests to bypass the legislature and impose their will by initiatives that pretend to be popularly generated, but that, in fact, pursue the political agenda of an elite few. Some of the "reform" measures that have succeeded include the elimination of the inheritance tax, indexing the income tax, and cutting off state services to illegal immigrants. Among the most potentially disastrous were the initiatives mandating term limits.

A POLITICAL EARTHQUAKE

Proposition 140, which made the ballot in 1990, limited members of the assembly to six years, and senators to eight. The proposition was written by Pete Schabarum, a former Republican assemblyman and retired Los Angeles County supervisor who served a total of twenty-four years in public office before deciding that term limits were a good idea. Schabarum got some help in drafting the measure from several veterans of the Proposition 13 campaign. He also contributed more than $650,000 from his own campaign funds to hire a professional petition gatherer to get the necessary signatures to put Proposition 140 on the ballot.

In addition to term limits, Proposition 140 included some provisions that can be seen only as punishing the legislature and hobbling both its effectiveness and its attractiveness. The budget for legislative staff was cut by 40 percent, effective immediately. What was once considered the best legislative staff in the country was decimated, forcing many talented and skilled professionals out of public service. And the generous pension program for legislators was eliminated entirely, ensuring that the California state legislature will be comprised of more "citizen legislators," that is, the independently wealthy, who often are even more disconnected from the problems facing middle-class families than the people they will replace.

There were actually two term limit proposals on the 1990 ballot. Proposition 131 would have imposed twelve-year term limits on members of the state senate and assembly, along with a strict spending limit and partial public funding of campaigns. This proposition, however, limited only consecutive terms, allowing legislators to sit out a term and then return to office repeatedly.

Proposition 140 won by a narrow margin, 52 to 48 percent. While the initiative was hotly contested and given great play in both the free and paid media, voter turnout was abysmally low. The majority that restricted every voter's choice of state legislators made up less than 20 percent of the eligible voters of the state. At the same time, Proposition 131 was defeated by a 62 to 38 percent margin.

The term limits and staff cuts of Proposition 140 were upheld by the California supreme court. But the court struck down the pension elimination as unconstitutional.

Two years later, Proposition 164 made the ballot. It limited congressional representatives to six years of service within eleven years and kept senators from serving more than twelve years within any seventeen years. Proposition 164 was funded by U.S. Term Limits, a national group that backs term limits legislation in many states. The so-called grassroots organization gave at least $600,000 to California groups supporting Proposition 164, $500,000 of that within little more than a week, according to a study by California Common Cause.[2]

Proposition 164 won with 62 percent of the vote. Simultaneously, Californians voted to return all but three congressional incumbents running in the general election. Clearly, they were happy with their own representatives, but they wanted to term limit everyone else's.

WHO LOSES?

Since Proposition 140 was passed in 1990 and imposed a six-year nonretroactive limit on state senators and members of the assembly, California is the first state in which we will see the results of term limits. Many of the consequences will be a long time coming. But already there have been some direct and, sadly, predictable results.

Almost immediately after the initiative was upheld in court, there was a scramble among state legislators for new jobs. Many quit their positions in midterm, costing their local governments millions of dollars for special elections in order to fill the empty seats. The revolving door between public service and private interest is spinning fast in Sacramento, as legislators jockey for lobbying positions with the very industries about whom they had once written negatively affecting legislation. Others are running for different state legislative offices, as the California law allows them to serve a total of fourteen years between the assembly and senate. Still others are opting out of politics altogether, dispirited by a system that no longer works.

There is another problem. As David Broder says about California, "Too many people are running for too many offices."[3] In the 1992 primary there were 21 people running for 2 U.S. Senate seats and 286 people running for 52 U.S. House positions. After redistricting created a new House seat near San Diego, 15 candidates were on the primary ballot. While competition is good for democracy, this cross-es into the realm of chaos. And having fields this crowded makes it much easier for fringe or extreme candidates to win a place on the ballot with pluralities of 20 or 30 percent of the vote.

At the state level, term limits have added to this electoral over-load. Looking at term limits in their near futures, thirty-one of the hundred state senators and members of the assembly are quitting or running for other offices. Term limits have created an almost 33 percent turnover, even before officially taking effect.

The California state government is huge, with a $55 billion bud-get and 128 different departments and agencies. And it's in trouble. "Were California a corporation, it would have little option but to ini-tiate some sort of bankruptcy proceeding," says John Vasconcellos, chairman of the State Assembly Ways and Means Committee. If you were a stockholder in a company that faced bankruptcy, would you want it run by a group of inexperienced businessmen who knew that they weren't going to be with the company much longer and wouldn't have to answer for the long-term consequences of their actions?

WHO WINS?

Is this the kind of chaos and flux that we want in a representative democracy? New blood is necessary in order to keep a legislative body innovative and responsive. But artificially enforced change resulting in such massive turnover (and, remember, term limits haven't even taken effect yet) can only bring about confusion and a power vacuum. Since politics abhors a vacuum, some other group is going to assume the power that the legislature will lose. With the legislative staff cut almost in half and the governor also term-limited, guess who'll take over the state?

Special interests, especially lobbyists representing major indus-tries, are already a preeminent force in California politics. Even before term limits, the government was becoming increasingly frac-tured and gridlocked. As a result, lobbyists will effectively control the government. Douglas Foster of Stanford University describes what's already happening and can only get worse. "Lobbyists are now writing more speeches for members, and are even drafting legislation themselves. Increasingly, they are referred to openly as 'sponsors' of new laws."[4]

Special interest lobbies are growing more powerful, not only by dealing with the now weakened and inexperienced legislature, but by taking their case directly to the people. "Astroturf" campaigns, in which citizens themselves are lobbied by moneyed interests to create the facade of a grassroots uprising, are increasingly common. "Phone mail, personal contact, public-relations programs at the grassroots—that's what we'll see in the future," says superlobbyist George Steffes, who represents some of the state's largest oil, finance, and insurance companies.[5]

These new lobbying techniques are harder to monitor and could prove to be very effective. Powerful special interests have already learned how to manipulate the initiative process to pass laws over the heads of the legislators, laws that will benefit their industries.

This two-pronged approach to lobbying—controlling a weakened legislature and launching a massive personal relations campaign directly to the people—is sure to make lobbyists much more powerful than they already are. While term limits were sold to Californians as a way to increase their voice in government, the result has been less power to the people.

Steffes sums up the lobbyists' perspective this way: "Make the rules, and I'll win. Whatever your rules are, I'm going to win."[6]

Some lobbyists are less Machiavellian. Foster cornered a lobbyist for insurance companies who didn't seem very enthusiastic about term limits. He asked the lobbyist why he wasn't celebrating.

"The fact is," the unnamed lobbyist said, "I realize that my clients are not always right. With a strong legislature, there's a balance of forces. You make your argument, fight for your client's position, and you have a chance to prevail if you've also got a case on the merits. But nobody should get everything they want.... Sometimes, you know, your client doesn't deserve to win."[7]

A lobbyist is like a trial lawyer, arguing the strongest case he can and using the facts to his best advantage. In court, a jury hears *both* sides so it can make an informed, sound, and fair decision. The judge makes sure that both the plaintiff and defendant have the opportunity to make their case and that the arguments are within legal and ethical bounds. In many ways, the legislature acts as the adjudicator of the claims of special interests, some of whom are in concert, others in conflict. By weakening the California legislature, term limits have diminished this judicial capacity and allowed the advocates with the most money to make the rules.

A COMATOSE GOVERNMENT

One issue that in many ways typifies the problems of the California legislature is Rep. Stan Statham's proposal to divide California into three separate states. Statham is no eccentric back-bencher; he's the assembly's senior Republican. The debate over Statham's proposal was a mix of quirky demagoguery, with politicians quoting Moses ("Let my people go"); complaints that some don't want to wind up in the same state as "those weirdos in San Francisco"; and somber prognostications (one legislator compared a Balkanized California to Yugoslavia).

The measure did not pass. But the method behind it illustrates much of what is now wrong with California politics. First of all, it shows the triviality of what passes for politics in a term-limited state. With little institutional memory and no long-term commitment, legislators propose and debate issues of increasing marginality and symbolism rather than addressing more substantive, difficult, and pressing issues. Even worse, Statham did not propose legislation but an initiative, leaving the ultimate decision of whether California should be split into three states up to the people themselves, rather than the legislators they elected to represent them. This was a curious abdication of power by the legislature. Instead of deliberating an issue and making a decision, the legislature took the easy way out. If the initiative got on the ballot and passed and a divided California proved disastrous, the legislature wouldn't be at fault.

Statham himself put his finger on the problem: "State government is in a coma, to put it politely."

A CAUTIONARY TALE

Of course, term limits are not the only problem plaguing the Golden State. But term limits are making it impossible to deal politically with the real problems. And the measures that imposed term limits are part of a larger problem: initiatives are increasingly being used to bypass the legislature and make laws that reflect the interest of a favored few who have massive amounts of money to outspend the opposition.

California prides itself on being ahead of the curve. In many ways it is the future of America, the place where our country begins again. If that is the case, we should learn from California's mistakes in the same way that we have emulated its successes. With California's term limits, however, we see not some new beginning, but the decline of functioning democracy. If term limits were passed on a national level, they would have the same crippling effects: a weakened government, hobbled by chaotic politics and controlled by special interests, unable to address the serious problems that face a troubled people.

Term limits will Californicate the rest of America.

Chapter 6

Laboratories of Chaos

Term limits are like clear-cutting old forests. They don't bother the underbrush much, but they're hell on the tall timber.
—T. K. Wetherell, Speaker of the Florida House

BEFORE THE SUPREME COURT upheld *U.S. Term Limits v. Thornton* on May 22, 1995, effectively erasing all state-imposed federal term limits legislation from the lawbooks, twenty-three states had voted for some kind of term limitations on their congressional representatives. All but two of them, however—Alaska and North Dakota—also limited the terms of their state legislators, and these laws are not affected by the high court's decision. And several hundred cities, from Anchorage to Jacksonville, from Honolulu to Atlanta, have imposed term limits on their elected officials. While it's still too early to fully measure the consequences of this orgy of legislation fully, term limits have already begun to change the way our states and cities operate and have become a significant factor in elections.

In every form of political change there are consequences, both intended and unintended, predictable and unpredictable. Term limits are no different. Many supporters of national term limits are looking to the states and municipalities to act as laboratories of democracy that will make state- and citywide term limits the model for like measures at the federal level.

Term limiters have promised us nothing less than a renewed democracy, operated by citizen legislators able to rise above the corruption, personal interest, and political ambition that tainted the process in those dark days of unlimited terms. Like all political promises, it offers more than it could ever possibly deliver. Like too many political promises we've heard recently, it's a cynical distortion of reality.

BACK TO THE BEGINNING

Term limiters complain that state legislatures have become too professionalized. A generation ago, the problem with state legislatures was that they were not professional enough.

In those days, too many state legislatures consisted of part-time jobs with part-time pay, very little institutional power, and negligible staff. One of the major problems facing statehouses was a high rate of turnover. During the 1930s, about half of all state legislators were rookies. That situation improved somewhat by the 1960s, when approximately two out of every five state legislators were serving their first terms.

In the 1960s, states across the country began reform movements to increase the power of the legislatures and to attract more capable leaders to elective office. All over the country, state houses increased salaries, established pension systems, lengthened sessions, built new offices, and hired staffers to work in them. Several large states even went to a full-time system, with regular sessions meeting most of the year.

These changes were necessary, given that so many federal responsibilities have been transferred to the states in the past twenty years. They attracted a new breed of politician to state capitals—one capable of dealing in policy substance—and made the job of legislator more than just one way of attracting business to one's law practice. By all accounts, the modernization of state legislatures is a success. One measure of this success is the degree to which congressional Republicans are anxious to devolve more and more federal programs and functions to the states. Perhaps Congress will learn a few lessons about how to run a legislative body by observing some state houses in action.

Unfortunately, no one has noticed. "The irony is that legislatures are doing a better job than ever, but getting less and less credit for it," says Alan Rosenthal, a political scientist at Rutgers University.[1]

Much of the anger felt by the voters that had been directed at Congress and the president is now directed toward their own state legislatures. The result is a series of term limits laws that can only be described as punitive in nature, and the election of a new kind of legislator, loyal not to the institution but to him- or herself. This new kind of legislator is eager to support and propose legislative gimmicks—like term limits if the state doesn't already have them, or increased term limits if it does—rather than take substantive steps to actually solve the problems angry voters face back home. "Time was, when part of our responsibility was to protect the institution of the legislature and maintain its integrity. That seems to have been forgotten." So says Ted Strickland, Colorado senate president. Unfortunately, Strickland, a capable leader who respects his institution and his role in it, has to leave office in a few years.

TURNOVER IN THE STATES

Even if we grant the term limiters their dubious argument that more turnover means a better legislature, term limits are unnecessary and counterproductive. In fact, term limits may actually decrease turnover in most legislatures.

Let's take a look at the first three states to pass term limits laws. The National Conference of State Legislatures (NCSL) studied the legislatures of Oklahoma, Colorado, and California and determined that the lower houses of all three state legislatures had a turnover rate of 89 percent or more from 1977 to 1989. During the same period, 74 percent or more of the senate seats in Oklahoma and Colorado and 67 percent of California's senate seats changed hands. In a single year, Colorado experienced a 24 percent turnover in both houses, while Oklahoma's was 30 percent.[2]

Since term limits are just now taking effect, it is impossible to gauge as yet what level of turnover they will generate. California certainly had a great initial turnover, as some thirty out of one hundred assembly members and senators quit their offices or refused to run again once the law was upheld by the state supreme court. But the two other states have legislatures with historically high turnovers, which leads one to wonder why their citizens voted for term limits in the first place.

Following Lloyd Noble's term limits initiative in Oklahoma (see chapter 1), incumbents ironically faced even fewer challenges. The 1992 elections in that state saw thirty-nine incumbents ensure their victory before the general election, either by running unopposed or by defeating their only competition in the primary and then facing no opponents in the general. Two years later, forty-nine incumbents were reelected unopposed. Once term limits go into effect, even more incumbents will probably walk to victory in unopposed races. The reason? Challengers say, "Why run against an incumbent when the seat will be vacant in a few years?" By passing a term limits law, Oklahoma guaranteed less competitive elections.

Nationwide, turnover in state senates between 1979 and 1989 was 72.9 percent. In lower houses it was 74.68 percent, according to a study by the NCSL. In 1994 alone, 23 percent of all state legislative seats up for election changed hands. In most of the twenty-three states that have adopted term limits laws, there will be a 100 percent turnover within eight to twelve years. That's not much more new talent (a term used loosely) than would enter the legislatures under normal circumstances, and it deprives the bodies of their most able and experienced members.

Leadership is essential, both in the part-time legislatures, which are often filled with inexperienced politicians, and in the professional statehouses, in which complex legislation and labyrinthine state bureaucracies are often beyond the grasp of neophytes. To retire experienced legislators automatically is to deprive the states of their most capable leaders. Much of the renaissance of state governments is due to these great legislators, and the institutions can only decline after their forced departure.

WHO STAYS, WHO GOES?

Term limiters are willing to cut down the tall trees in order to clear out the scrub brush. Unfortunately, the best people are often the first to go.

An editorial in the *Sacramento Bee* stated that the immediate result of term limits has "not been to drive out the hacks and the ideologues, much less to reduce the institutional venality, but to discourage precisely those who have worked hardest and most conscientiously to be good legislators."[3]

A system that does not reward effectiveness or seniority will attract people of lower quality or suspect motivations and discourage those with good intentions. Politicians are people just like you and me; they have desires and ambitions, but they also react to incentives and disincentives. Term limits create disincentives that make it difficult for good legislators to persevere, while at the same time putting in place a host of incentives for political irresponsibility.

LEGISLATURES AND GOVERNORS

Term limits on state legislators adversely tip the scales of power toward the executive branch. In many states the governor's office itself is term-limited. But in these states the chief executive often wields more power relative to the legislature than does the president relative to Congress. Any weakening of the legislative branch will strengthen the executive, not to mention the permanent government of bureaucrats and the quasi government of lobbyists.

State governments have a balance of power that closely resembles the constitutional system of checks and balances. Reducing legislative authority would make the governor a preeminent force.

Alan Rosenthal of Rutgers University says that under term limits "it will be up to the governors to advance a program and pull the legislature together even to a greater degree than they do today. The legislature will be the weak branch of government."[4]

Since the legislature is the closest branch of government to the people, it is important that that body remain powerful in order for the people's voice to be heard. Limiting the terms of state legislators is one sure way to diminish democracy and reduce the participation that individuals have in their own government.

Rosenthal notes that along with gubernatorial dominance comes bureaucratic dominance. "The government will be ruled by bureaucrats building up their programs and their budgets without having to contend with strong legislatures. That will be a splendid irony for those advocates of term limits who prefer a small government."[5]

MUNICIPAL TERM LIMITS

Term limits on the local level are not always quite so troubling. More than two thousand municipalities have some form of term limits, but these laws often can be rescinded or modified more easily than those that apply statewide. Once voters realize the folly of term limits, they can change the laws back to the way they were. In some places it has already happened.

The town of South Pasadena, Florida, passed a law ten years ago requiring that all members of its city commission be limited to three consecutive three-year terms. Last year Fred Held, a city commissioner who had served his nine years, dutifully left his office the day his last term expired.

The very next day, Held got a phone call from the city clerk. She needed his help. It seemed that the four commissioners now serving had a combined total of four years experience, and they had no idea what they were doing. So they had a meeting and came up with a great idea: they'd ask Fred to come back.

Although the law had stipulated that you couldn't serve more than nine years in a row, it said nothing at all about how long you had to be out of office before you could return. As far as the four city commissioners were concerned, Held's one-day sabbatical was plenty long enough.

Two days after leaving office under term limits, Held was unanimously elected mayor by the city commission. As Alan Ehrenhalt of *Governing* magazine pointed out, "His return increased the combined total of government experience by 550 percent."[6]

Little damage can be done by a few city commissioners in a small town inhabited mostly by retirees. But what's going to happen to New York City, where politics are chaotic under normal circumstances, when term limits for the city council begin taking effect? How will San Francisco's fractious supervisors act when that city's term limits law kicks in? Can you imagine New Orleans run by a bunch of lame ducks?

Term limits at the local level is often motivated by partisan politics. Take, for example, Cobb County, Georgia. Just a couple of years ago, Republican Newt Gingrich's home district was represented by Democrats in the statehouse, but Republican county commissioners controlled local politics. So the state legislators proposed term limits on county officials. You can bet that Newt, who is getting to like term limits less and less the more they stare him in the face, wasn't too thrilled with that proposal.

And, of course, Cobb County has no need for term limits. Three different chairs have led the commission in the past ten years, and no commissioner has gotten close to the eight years that would push him or her out of office. As one Cobb County politician put it, "The suburbs eat their young."

The only extensive study of municipal term limits that we know of was conducted by John David Rausch, who is something of a one-man industry of term limits scholarship. He took a look at the effects of term limits on supervisors in San Mateo County, California, and found there was even less electoral competitiveness and lower voter turnout than before. In the first election after term limits took effect, two seats were open. Two candidates ran, both unopposed. That's as uncompetitive as it gets. Voter turnout, moreover, began decreasing as soon as term limits were passed and continues to decline now that they have taken effect.[7]

A PUNITIVE ACTION

If term limits are so disastrous, why did so many people vote for them?

Rausch suggests that voters support term limits simply because it makes them feel good. "Through term limits, voters are able to 'punish' the legislature without punishing individual legislators."[8] If that is the case, then the price for term limits politics, like any other feel-good measure, will be a great deal of pain for only a moment of pleasure.

People are angry and frustrated with government, and are eager to see a change in the way things are run. They are voting for term limits for the same reason that they gave so many incumbents their walking papers in the last election—to send a message. But there's a difference between turning out an incumbent and enacting a law that disables the body politic. Supporters of term limits should realize that it is one thing to protest, quite another to tear down. Term limits are more than mere symbolism. In twenty states and hundreds of municipalities, they're now the law.

Chapter 7

Are Elections Necessary?

I'm tired of hearing it said that democracy doesn't work. Of course it doesn't work. It isn't supposed to work. We are supposed to work it.
—Alexander Woollcott

ELECTIONS ARE MORE than just a cornerstone of our democracy; they're the entire foundation. So when we start fiddling around with the electoral process, we risk damaging the very structure of our political system. And every change that we do make should enhance democracy, not cripple or diminish it. That's why we should consider very carefully the effects that term limits would have on elections.

Term limits fans say that their proposal will make elections more competitive and fair. By eliminating the power of incumbency, they argue, term limits will open up elections to new challengers. More competitive elections will create greater turnover. And greater turnover will result in better political leaders.

But, in fact, term limits will make elections less competitive, less fair, and, as we saw in the last chapter, will even reduce legislative turnover. Incumbents, though limited to a certain number of terms, will find reelection more of a breeze than before. And large campaign contributions, especially from political action committees (PACs), will increasingly benefit sitting politicians and make a successful challenge even more difficult than it is today.

A close examination of the 1986, 1988, and 1990 elections in this chapter reveals that incumbency is not so big a problem as it may seem. And a look at the 1992 and 1994 races in the next chapter will show that the electorate is certainly willing and able to generate plenty of natural turnover in office without term limits.

A PERMANENT CONGRESS?

The term limits movement started to gain popular support after the elections of 1986 and 1988, in which incumbents were reelected at a rate of about 98 percent. This short-lived phenomenon created a lot of sound bites, as activists railed against a "permanent Congress," arguing that term limits were the only way to challenge incumbency effectively.

But nothing is ever as simple as a sound bite makes it seem. There are two points to make about the rate of incumbency return: It is neither as bad nor as unprecedented as it sounds. And the problem isn't incumbency, it's money.

A significant, and often forgotten, reason for high incumbency return is that many constituents actually like their representatives and approve of their performance in office. It should be remembered that the person in office was originally elected because the voters believed that he or she could best represent their interests. So long as the representative performs according to the voters' expectations, it would be surprising if he or she were defeated. While incumbents should not have an unfair advantage over challengers, neither should they be penalized or scorned for doing their jobs well or carrying out the wishes of their constituents.

In the 1980s, there was a general trend to reelect running incumbents. During this time of economic expansion, many, if not all, in